5 EASY STEPS
TO SPEAK SPANISH
WITH CONFIDENCE

BECOME CONVERSATIONAL
IN 3 MONTHS OR LESS

DAVID E STEVENS III

CONTENTS

INTRODUCTION

A Letter From The Author

Hola amigo,

I am very excited that you have found The Language School and I can't wait to share with you these *5 Easy Steps to Speak Spanish with Confidence*. If you follow this plan and work the steps, you will be speaking Spanish conversationally in 3 months or less.

But before we get started on this amazing adventure together, I want to ask you something:

If you have tried to learn how to speak Spanish before, do these situations sound familiar?

- I signed up for classes but I gave up – it was too frustrating.
- I can't memorize the words. I try, but it is too difficult.
- I tried Rosetta Stone but I wasn't disciplined enough and I had too many questions.
- My biggest problem is with doubt – I don't have any confidence with what I am saying.
- There are so many words and phrases – I never know what is correct.

- I have tried to practice by myself, but I always get bored. What can I do to keep moving forward?

If any of these resonated with you I want you to plan on dedicating 10-15 minutes everyday for the next 10 days so that speaking Spanish becomes much easier for you!

Here is an email that one of my students just sent me:

> *"I've been working on lesson 2. I'll admit that it was a little intimidating when we went over it together at school. But, I did like you said. I followed your advice. It actually went very well. I'm really enjoying the experience."*

Regardless of your level of Spanish, these concepts will dramatically improve your conversational skills in just a couple of weeks. If you continue, in only 3 months you should be able to talk to Spanish speakers in 85% of your daily activities and become fully fluent in 6 months.

Look, learning Spanish doesn't have to be complicated, difficult, or stressful. *It should be easy, fun, and entertaining!*

My mission in life is dedicated to this. I am so excited to help you get started that I have also created a special email series with free tutorials to accompany this book. You can sign up for it online at no cost by visiting the following link:

http://www.thelanguageschool.us/go/5-easy-steps-to-speak-spanish-with-confidence/

I believe that Spanish is powerful and can help you go farther both personally and professionally in the United States and around the world. I believe that everyone should have access to what speaking Spanish offers.

But I also understand that most people start learning Spanish in a way that makes it difficult and frustrating.

It is easy to get lost in the thousands of words, grammar rules, and verb conjugations. The majority of schools and teachers don't have a good conversational program and at the end of the day they make learning Spanish too complicated, impractical, or boring.

I know this because I went through this when I learned how to speak Spanish.

When I started to study Spanish I felt frustrated, irritated, and I almost quit studying. I had travelled to Spain for an immersion program and I was overwhelmed.

My teacher didn't speak a word of English and I couldn't understand her. Instead of focusing on common situations, we were learning grammar and tenses and I was completely confused.

Part of it was my fault - I wanted to understand everything right off the bat and speak it perfectly, instead of having fun and recognizing everything that I had actually accomplished.

Something had to change.

So I created my own program to make learning Spanish easy and fun and within a few weeks I was able to speak Spanish with much more confidence.

Now, over 15 years later, my *Let's Start Talking*

program has taught thousands of people how to speak both Spanish and English. Because of learning the new languages, they have been able to

- make more money
- make new friends
- have more confidence during their travels

Imagine how well you could speak Spanish if you didn't have to make the mistakes that I made.

You could start speaking with confidence in little time, helping you create a positive change in your life and your family's life too. Instead of being frustrated you could access your potential, which will help increase your passion for learning Spanish.

So I want to save you time and energy during your adventure to the Spanish speaking world and I will share with you *5 Easy Steps To Speaking Spanish With Confidence*.

I wrote this book because I truly want you to be successful with Spanish and I know that you can do it!

So, are you ready for an excellent trip into the Spanish-speaking world together with me? I am absolutely ready!

Continue reading for the first of the *5 Easy Steps To Speaking Spanish With Confidence*.

Saludos,

Tu amigo

David Stevens

Director of The Language School
Author, *Let's Start Talking*

PS: I love meeting my new students. Visit my Facebook page and like it. You will also get access to fun activities and a community with people like you.

Like it here:
https://www.facebook.com/TheLanguageSchool/

About The Language School

The Language School is an English/Spanish school with locations in Denver, Boulder and Longmont, Colorado, focused on providing excellent service to help students learn how to speak their new language. We use a unique and practical methodology, which ensures that students learn how to talk as soon as possible. Founded in 2007, The Language School has taught thousands of people how to speak a new language. This helps our students enrich their lives with better opportunities in their work environments, communication in their communities, and reduce or eliminate the frustration of living in a new place without speaking the new language.

Our services include:

- **Classes For Adults**
- **Specialized Lessons (Tutoring)**
- **International Business Services**
- **Immersion**

Providing a good education is our mission to help people who want to integrate into new cultures, achieve their goals, and remove the obstacles of not speaking or understanding new languages.

Our teachers are experts in teaching. They are experienced in teaching English and Spanish, so we can ensure that your education at The Language School will be successful.

For more information, contact:

http://www.thelanguageschool.us/
info@thelanguageschool.us

Phone: 303.997.9207

4730 Oakland St
Suite 200
Denver, CO 80239

Write About Your Objectives and Inspiration

Are you ready for our very first of the *5 Easy Steps to Speak Spanish with Confidence*?

Today's lesson is very important and easy to do, and if done, it will help you focus your goals, get inspired, and start learning conversational Spanish that is relevant to your daily life.

This will set you up for success for the life of your Spanish studies and you will be speaking Spanish with confidence very soon. And take it from me, someone that really struggled with learning Spanish, **this simple step worked wonders for me.**

My story...
Let's take a step back in time -
back to our teenage years...

If you were anything like me, chances are that you were in a high school Spanish class. The class was full with about 30 rowdy and rambunctious teenagers, bursting with hormones, who would rather have been anywhere but in Spanish class.

The teacher didn't want to be there any more than the students, and there is a good chance he or she didn't really speak Spanish. Going around the room, the teacher called on the students to say a single word in Spanish, and there were a few class clowns that would always find a way to make fun of the person that was really trying. *With this environment, how could anyone really be expected to start speaking Spanish?*

Later, I found myself in a situation where I realized that **I needed to learn how to speak Spanish**. I had just graduated from high school and returned from my senior trip to Spain and Paris. I was living in an apartment building and all of my neighbors were from Mexico. I was working on a construction project and most of the people that I worked with were from south of the border and spoke almost no English. ***Out of necessity, I had to learn how to speak Spanish.***

So, like anyone would have done in this position, I got on a plane and headed to Spain, enrolling in a full immersion program. **The best way to learn is by full immersion, right? WRONG!**

I didn't understand anything that was going on around me, and my teacher, who didn't speak any English, couldn't explain Spanish to me in a way that I could understand. You can't imagine how frustrated I started to feel.

I was at the point of giving up, going home early, and never speaking Spanish again, when I decided to do this - I sat down and wrote out my reasons for wanting to learn Spanish:

1. I want to be able to talk to my neighbors.
2. I want a Spanish-speaking girlfriend. (Let's be honest – Latin people are gorgeous!)
3. I want to travel all over Latin America and experience things I have always dreamed of!
4. I want to be able to talk to everyone that I work with.
5. I want to put that I am bilingual on a resume so I can become more competitive in the job market.
6. I want to be flexible with where I work and be able to work in other countries.

This really helped me understand that I had a genuine desire to learn how to speak Spanish, and I knew that I couldn't give up! **Then I stopped being so concerned with understanding everything that was happening, and instead I started focusing on the things that I had learned.**

I had been in Spain for about 2 weeks, and I had learned how to order food and order drinks. I had learned how to introduce myself to people. I had learned how to go into a store and buy something.

And then it hit me – I don't have to speak the entire language – I just have to learn certain dialogues. So I started keeping a journal of my daily experiences, and more importantly, the conversations that I wish that I could have with people. Writing these little dialogues out helped me get organized and focused on what I needed to learn, and I recommend that everyone learning Spanish do the same.

What do you say when you meet someone for the first time? You introduce yourself and tell them where you are from. You ask them what they like to do for fun and what kind of music they listen to. You talk about your friends and family, and what you do for work. So while my teacher was going on and on in class about verb conjugations and sentence structure, I realized that I needed to focus on learning how to make small talk.

About a week later, my third week in Spain, I had my first conversation with someone. I was returning home from Las Ramblas, an area in Barcelona filled with bars and restaurants, and got in a cab with a non English-speaking cabbie. **We talked the entire time in Spanish during my 15-minute ride home**, and I didn't even realize it until I went upstairs and got in bed. Just before dozing off, I jumped up with excitement because I realized that I had finally started speaking Spanish!

So, if you don't have a Spanish journal, then start one now! Your Spanish journal is a place where you can store your ideas, dialogues, vocabulary and thoughts about Spanish. You can use it, like I did, to make notes about the conversations you have and the ones you want to have.

The magic of this activity is that it starts the process of making Spanish *relevant*. You are taking what is most helpful for you as you learn how to speak Spanish, and you're turning it into something that has meaning for YOU. You're not just relying on what 'the book/ teacher' says - you're relying on what your experiences say.

Activity 1

Step 1: Find a notebook.

It doesn't have to be anything fancy, just simply something that has paper that you can take with you wherever you go. Make it yours and decorate it with pictures of Spanish speaking people and places that you want to visit.

Step 2: Divide your journal into sections.

Here are a few ideas for what sections you may want to create in your Spanish journal:

- **Dialogues**- start with the end in mind – write down a typical conversation that you would have in English with someone. Then try to translate it into Spanish by looking up words in a dictionary. Google is actually pretty good about translating a phrase by typing in "How do you say _____ in Spanish?"

- **Vocabulary**- as you write down your dialogues, try to classify them by topics of conversation and extract vocabulary. For example, if you are writing about ordering food at a restaurant, start collecting a list of words related to food and drinks. Even if you can't speak a complete sentence, telling a waiter the word "bistec" will get a steak delivered to your table.

- **Conversation starters**- Think about how you might start a conversation with a colleague at work. Do you like baseball? Nice day today, huh! Do you have any kids? Chances are, these will work in Spanish too. Having a list of conversation starters prepared will help you break the ice! Check out my book, <u>Let's Start Talking: A bilingual book for English and Spanish students!</u> on Amazon for as low as $4.99 (kindle version).

- **Personal reflection** – As you start speaking Spanish, write about your experiences. What worked? What didn't work? What do you wish you could have said? Remember to always congratulate yourself on your small victories and instead of getting frustrated by what you couldn't say, use that as motivation and build your vocabulary!

Step 3: Start writing.

If you can, bring your journal with you and write about your experiences as soon as possible after speaking with people so that the dialogues are fresh in your mind. Later in the day before sleeping, or first thing in the morning, try to translate these conversations. If you do this for 10-15 minutes a day, you should be speaking Spanish in just a couple of weeks!

Use the following pages to help you get started.

People typically want to learn Spanish for personal or professional reasons, or a combination of both. Writing down your goals can help you feel motivated while you are learning how to speak Spanish.

Please take a few minutes to write down the reasons why you want to learn Spanish:

Personal

1.)_____

2.)_____

3.)_____

Professional

1.)_____

2.)_____

3.)_____

¡Muy bien! Very good! Now you know your reasons for studying, and you will have motivation to keep going forward. Now you should feel really good for deciding to take this huge step! Write down your feelings below!

Studying Spanish makes me feel:

_____

_____

_____

_____

_____

_____

_____

_____

Most importantly, keep tabs on your daily conversations, both personal and professional. This will help you make learning Spanish relevant, and will help you focus on learning the Spanish that you need to start speaking now! Use the worksheet on the following page and try to do this for the next ten days.

Example:

I:	Hi honey. How are you?
Yo:	Hola amor. ¿Cómo estás?
My wife:	I'm good. What do you want for dinner?
Mi esposa:	Estoy bien. ¿Qué deseas para la cena?
I:	I'm hungry. I want a steak and a salad.
Yo:	Tengo hambre. Deseo un bistec y una ensalada.
My wife:	Do you want to drink wine with that?
Mi esposa:	¿Deseas tomar vino con eso?
I:	Yes, good idea. Thanks, I love you.
Yo:	Si, buen idea. Gracias, te quiero.
My wife:	I love you too!
Mi esposa:	¡Te quiero también!

Conversation Guidelines:

1. **Real conversations**
2. **Relevant**
3. **Practical**

Notice that the conversation is very simple and short, but it is 100% practical and relevant to your daily life. Depending on your level of Spanish, you can keep the conversations simple or add complexity to them.

Now you try!

I: _____

Yo: _____

My wife: _____

Mi esposa: _____

I: _____

Yo: _____

My wife: _____

Mi esposa: _____

I: _____

Yo: _____

My wife: _____

Mi esposa: _____

EASY STEP #2:

Learn 10 New Words A Day

Hola – Hello
Gracias – Thanks
Por Favor – Please
De Nada – You're Welcome

In the first step I taught you the importance of using a Spanish journal to build your personal connection to the Spanish language and to make it fun and relevant.

How is it going? Have you started journaling?

I promise you that the more you work with your journal to help define your personal goals with Spanish, the faster you will be able to speak Spanish with confidence!

Now, are you ready for Step 2? Yes!!! ¡Si!

Before we get started let me share with you a story about when I was struggling to master the Spanish language and the one thing that saved me hours of study every day.

I started my Spanish studies in 2001 when I was 18, right after graduating high-school. I wasn't really sure about going to college yet, but I knew that I wanted to become fluent in Spanish and travel the world.

I enrolled in an immersion program in Spain. I had limited success with the official program at that school. Later, I enrolled in a Spanish program at the University of Colorado and started by just taking night classes 2 days a week.

Being a successful Spanish student in college meant spending an excessive amount of time working with a Spanish grammar textbook (and spending even more money on the book), memorizing grammar rules and verb conjugations. It also meant spending hours on fill in the blank activities and working through multiple-choice answers.

But there was a big problem with this. There was no conversation!

Why do you want to learn Spanish? Are people going to send you emails with several choices to reply? No, of course not! **You want to learn Spanish to speak it!**

Initially I worked the college program, and I fumbled my way through the homework, guessing most of the time. But I wanted to speak Spanish, not guess it.

What I ultimately learned was that to be a better Spanish speaker, **I really needed to improve my vocabulary.** So I came up with a plan to study vocabulary before doing my homework. I realized that by memorizing new words, I didn't really need to know the grammar and verb conjugations that the professor was so concerned with. I could start piecing together conversations with my neighbors and people that I was working with simply by knowing words.

For example, think about the last time you spoke with someone that didn't really speak English very well. Here is a typical exchange:

- You: Do you like to eat pizza?
- Person from another country: Yes, me like pizza!

We can see the power of vocabulary in this exchange - the answer is completely incorrect grammatically, but you understand it. Now, don't get me wrong, I am not saying that grammar is not important, **I'm simply trying to get you to focus on what is powerful, which are the words that you know in Spanish**. The grammar and structure will come in time, but the words will help you understand people and be understood in the short term

I will never forget the power of this, because after I started doing this, my Spanish professor interrupted class one day and asked everyone to turn around and look at me. We had just taken an exam that I felt pretty good about, but when the whole class turned around to look at me, my face turned red and I became nervous.

"Class, look at David, because I am very proud to announce that for the first time in my 20 year career of teaching Spanish, David got a 100% on the exam!"

So what I am about to share with you is an incredibly easy and fast activity, but it will make learning Spanish so much easier and build your confidence quickly.

Activity 2

Step 1: Choose a topic.

If you have been keeping a journal, you should be able to review some of your recent conversations. In terms of relevance, some of the best topics would include the following:

1. Home
2. School
3. Work

4. Family
5. Food
6. Sports
7. Fun activities
8. Chores
9. Places
10. Travel

Step 2: Add 10 words related to the topic.

Take a look at one of the topics. Write down the first ten words that come to mind.

Step 3: Look up the words in a dictionary.

You can even ask Google "how do you say _____ in Spanish?" and you will get an answer.

Step 4: Make flashcards

These are very useful to help you learn Spanish and memorize new vocabulary. Before doing homework, you should first memorize new vocabulary. By memorizing new words you can at least understand the context of a conversation.

In the 10+ years that I have been teaching Spanish, I have worked with a lot of students that were struggling with new vocabulary. If something else works for you – then do that, but I can guarantee that this simple and fast activity will work. I teach students how to do this and they all dramatically improve – if they do this activity as is written below.

Buy a pack of 3" X 5" index cards – they're available on Amazon for less than a dollar, or you can check at your local grocery store. Write down the new words that you want to learn on one side of the cards and write down the Spanish version on the other side.

This is how to use these flashcards:

1.) Put the flashcards in your hands so you can see the side written in Spanish.
2.) Review them, saying the Spanish word aloud.
3.) Try to say out loud what it means in English.
4.) If you say it correctly, put it off to the side. If you say it wrong, replace it in the back of the stack you have in your hands.
5.) Do this exercise until you know the meaning of all the words correctly.
6.) Now do the same, but in reverse (see the side written in English and say the word in Spanish).

Extra: Try to spell them too!

If you do this exercise before going to sleep and when you wake up, you'll be able to memorize and start using new vocabulary immediately.

If you need some extra help with this check out my book Let's start talking: Spanish Foundations: A beginner's level guide to speaking Spanish, available on Amazon for $30. It is loaded with vocabulary and even includes flashcards that you can cut out!

This simple, 5-minute exercise literally changed the way I studied Spanish because it was a practical approach and was extremely efficient.

By doing this daily you will keep Spanish fresh in your mind, which will allow you to speak it and understand it faster. Pretty soon you will start understanding words here and there and then the context of conversations, which will keep you excited about the learning process.

Did you know that the 1000 most commonly used words make up 85% of daily communications? That means that if you do this activity, in 3 months you will know enough Spanish to cover yourself conversationally in the majority of your daily interactions.

Use this template to create your own custom vocab list, or use the suggested words on the following pages.

My custom vocabulary list

Palabras de _____/Words about _____

1. _____

2. _____

3. _____

4. _____

5. _____

6. _____

7. _____

8. _____

9. _____

10. _____

Day one:
Palabras de la casa/Words from home

1. Casa/House

2. Apartamento/Apartment

3. Cocina/Kitchen

4. Habitación/Bedroom

5. Baño/Bathroom

6. Sótano/Basement

7. Sala/Living Room

8. Comedor/Dining Room

9. Garaje/Garage

10. Patio/ Yard

Day two:
Palabras de la escuela/Words from school

1. Escuela/School

2. Salón de clase/Classroom

3. Lápiz/Pencil

4. Bolígrafo/Pen

5. Cuaderno/Notebook

6. Libro/Book

7. Mochila/Backpack

8. Pizarra/Whiteboard, Chalkboard

9. Maestro, Maestra/Teacher

10. Estudiante/ Student

Day three:
Palabras del trabajo/Words from work

1. Escritorio/Desk
2. Cubículo/Cubicle
3. Cocina/Kitchen
4. Salario/Salary
5. Oficina/Office
6. Entrevista/Interview
7. Sala de conferencia/Conference room
8. Gerente/Manager
9. Colega/Colleague
10. Patrón, Jefe/ Boss

Day four:
Palabras de la familia/Words about family

1. Abuelo/Grandpa
2. Abuela/Grandma
3. Tío/Uncle
4. Tía/Aunt
5. Esposo/Husband
6. Esposa/Wife
7. Hijo/Son
8. Hija/Daughter
9. Hermano/Brother
10. Hermana/ Sister

Day five:
Palabras de la comida/Words about food

1. Desayuno/Breakfast

2. Almuerzo/Lunch

3. Cena/Dinner

4. Carne/Meat, beef

5. Pollo/Chicken

6. Verduras/Vegetables

7. Fruta/Fruit

8. Bebidas/Drinks

9. Restaurante/Restaurant

10. Tengo hambre/I'm hungry

Day six:
Palabras de los deportes/Words about sports

1. Fútbol/Soccer

2. Fútbol americano/Football

3. Beisbol/Baseball

4. Baloncesto/Basketball

5. Árbitro/Referee

6. Jugador/Player

7. Falta/Foul

8. Director técnico/Coach

9. Lanzar/Shoot

10. Jugar/Play

Day seven:
Palabras de actividades divertidas/Words about fun activities

1. Jugar deportes/Play sports
2. Tocar música/Play music
3. Bailar/Dance
4. Cantar/Sing
5. Ir al cine/Go to the movies
6. Caminar en el parque/Walk in the park
7. Nadar/Swim
8. Convivir/Hang out
9. Tomar/Drink
10. Leer/Read

Day eight:
Palabras de los quehaceres/Words about chores

1. Pasar la aspiradora/Vacuum
2. Sacar la basura/Take out the trash
3. Limpiar/Clean
4. Trapear/Mop
5. Fregar los platos/Wash dishes
6. Lavar la ropa/Wash clothes
7. Cortar el césped/Cut the grass
8. Poner la mesa/Set the table
9. Ir al banco/Go to the bank
10. Pagar las cuentas/Pay the bills

Day nine:
Palabras de los lugares/Words about places

1. Correo/Post office

2. Banco/Bank

3. Gimnasio/Gym

4. Montañas/Mountains

5. Playa/Beach

6. Río/River

7. Campo/Countryside

8. Centro/Downtown

9. Barrio/Neighborhood

10. Tienda/Store

Day ten:
Palabras de viajar/Words about travel

1. Volar/Fly

2. Avión/Plane

3. Tren/Train

4. Carro/Car

5. Manejar/Drive

6. Subir/Board

7. Bajar/Get off, exit

8. Hotel/Hotel

9. Maletas/Bags, suitcases

10. Crucero/Cruise

EASY STEP #3:

Sign Up For Conversational Spanish Lessons

So if you have been working on your Spanish journal and learning 10 new Spanish words a day - you are doing great! Let's take it to the next level!

Today, I am going to share with you a very simple idea: how to sign up for conversational Spanish lessons with a trusted Spanish school like the school I started in Denver in 2007, The Language School. If you live close to Denver, we would love to have you here. But if you are somewhere else, then I am going to teach you how to find Spanish schools in your area and evaluate them so you can start speaking Spanish with confidence even faster.

Let's take a look at some fascinating information about the Spanish language…

The evolution of Spanish….

The Spanish language that is spoken today by over 500 million people around the world was born from Latin and can be traced all the way back to 210 BC. It is one of the romance languages, but you might not know that it is called a romance language because Latin came from Rome, not because it is romantic!

Back at this time, only the wealthy and elite people were able to learn how to read and write and most people in the Roman Empire began speaking dirty versions of Latin, and thus Spanish, French, Italian, and Portuguese were born.

Outside of Latin, Arabic has had the biggest influence on the Spanish language, and approximately 8% of the language has been borrowed from Arabic. This is because the Muslim Moors crossed the Straight of Gibraltar in the 700s and occupied Spain for about 700 years. From there, the Spanish language travelled to the New World and is the predominant language spoken in the Americas today.

Whether you live in the United States or Europe, Spanish is arguably the most important second language to study. With Spanish and English, you can easily travel throughout almost every continent in the world.

If you live in the US, speaking Spanish will enable you to meet more people and increase your job potential. Some people think that it may become the dominant language here over the next fifty years.

With such a long history, prolific spread around the globe, and good incentives to learn Spanish, you would think that it should be pretty easy to find a school and learn how to speak Spanish. After all, it is now a requirement to study for two years in both high school and college.

Wrong - most Spanish schools and programs do not focus on teaching students how to speak Spanish, but rather on grammar. They either go too fast or too slow. Frequently students feel overwhelmed or they get bored.

So why is this important? Spanish, just like any language, is a vast subject that practically has no limit to it, and finding a good program will be the difference in becoming fluent or giving up.

You need to find a Spanish program that will teach you the Spanish you need to survive in a new country (how to order food and find lodging) and Spanish that relates to your own personal goals (how to do business, make friends, talk to patients, etc.).

Think about your first language - how long have you been speaking it? Do you understand every word in the dictionary? Are you still learning it?

If you want to learn something simple like how to sharpen a pencil, it is pretty easy, because there is a very well defined starting and stopping point to this. But when learning a language, you have to be very well organized, understand your reasons, and come up with a good plan to start speaking immediately, otherwise you can quickly get overwhelmed and give up.

There is a good chance that if you are reading this that you had to study Spanish or another language at one point in time... so just think back to your high school or college days - why didn't you learn how to speak the language you studied?

The reason why most people that study Spanish are unsuccessful is because most programs are not the right combination of practical, fun, and easy. Most programs teach Spanish in the same way that a first language is taught, focusing on grammar.

But these programs are missing a huge point - people already know how to speak their first language by the time they start studying grammar. Learning grammar rules will help you perfect Spanish, but initially will not help you START speaking Spanish.

So let's learn how to evaluate schools so you can make a decision on where to study that is based on results. To start this process, I would like to share with you more about my path to speaking Spanish and the types of programs I tried.

1.) Immersion - My first experience with learning Spanish, outside of my high school classes, was through immersion. I thought that had to be the best, most powerful way to learn Spanish, so I headed straight to the source and flew to Barcelona, Spain.

However, I ran into several problems with this program - the course was taught by a woman that spoke no English and it was entirely taught in Spanish. I couldn't understand a word she said! I think immersion is a great way to learn Spanish if you are already some-what proficient, but if you are just getting started it can be incredibly frustrating to sit in a classroom for 1-4 hours at a time and not understand what your teacher is saying.

2.) University - My second experience with studying Spanish was to enroll at the University of Colorado. However, I ran into a few problems with this option as well. First, the focus of the class was on grammar. This is good for people that major in Spanish because they typically go on to teach Spanish, but it doesn't help most people that simply want to speak Spanish. Another setback was the size of the class - there were over 30 students in the classroom. The number 1 fear that most people have is public speaking - this is multiplied by 100 when your 2nd language is involved. Most college/university programs simply don't have programs that are geared towards making students feel comfortable speaking, and my goal was to speak the language.

3.) Software - I have tried programs like Rosetta Stone and Duolingo as well. I think software has it's place, and The Language School has even created an <u>app</u> to help students practice, but there are some major shortfalls with computer programs, again revolving around practical conversation. First, I had questions, but I couldn't ask my computer! Also, I never found the programs to be relevant to my personal goals. I didn't learn how to introduce myself or how to make small talk. I was learning a lot of vocabulary, but I wasn't speaking Spanish. Eventually I got bored with these apps and gave up. In conclusion, I thought these were good ways to practice Spanish but not really practical for learning how to speak it.

4.) Conversation partner - This was what I found to be the best way to meet my objectives of speaking Spanish. My first conversation partner was Juan, who had just moved to Colorado from Mexico. Juan was eager to learn English, and I was eager to learn Spanish. We started hanging out and teaching each other how to say things, and we were teaching each other real words and phrases that we needed to know to talk to each other and become friends.

The end result of my long and difficult journey is the good news for you - Today all across the United States language schools like the one I started are popping up to help people focus on conversational Spanish.

I hope that these stories are helping you understand the need to find a program that focuses on practical Spanish that you can start speaking from day one, which will greatly reduce your study time and the time it will take you to start speaking Spanish with confidence!

Activity 3

Spanish is a difficult language to learn by yourself with no outside help, and you are going to need to find a good place to teach the Spanish you want to know and that will provide you with the right support structure and help you find a conversation partner. You should look for a good Spanish school, like The Language School, and enroll. Use the checklist on the following pages to evaluate at least 2 schools before making a decision.

Look for Spanish schools in your city on Google. Make sure to look at their reviews on Google and Yelp too. Look for programs that have at least ten 4 star reviews and ensure some of the reviews are recent. If there are bad reviews, check to see if the owner has given a response before accepting it as a bad review. Then call them to learn about their programs.

Be careful and patient while making your choice – don't enroll in a school just because it is close to your house or because it is cheap. **You want a school that is going to give you results** and success with speaking the language.

Ask them these types of questions:

1. **How many students do you allow to enter the class?** You don't want to study in a class that has more than 10 people in it. More people mean less attention for you, and you simply won't get the attention that you need if the school works with large groups of students. This is the #1 reason that most high school and college programs fail to teach students how to speak Spanish today.

2. **What is the experience of the teachers?** You want a teacher that is an expert and professional. Just because someone speaks Spanish doesn't mean that they are qualified to teach Spanish. Those are two completely different talents.

3. **For whom are the classes?** If you are an adult it is not good to study with children, and vice versa. Adults learn differently and a program that mixes the two groups will result in frustrated students.

4. **What is the focus of the classes?** There are programs that focus on conversation, writing, grammar, reading, and other parts of the language. If you want to learn how to speak Spanish with confidence, you should look for a school that teaches conversational Spanish.

5. **Can I take an evaluation?** You want to be in a level with students that have the same experience/level as you. If not, someone will get frustrated. Before enrolling in a course, you want to take an evaluation to be sure that you are enrolling in the correct level and it's a professional school.

If a school responds well, then you can ask about the price. If you can pay it, do it, even if the price is a little high. Your education is priceless, and learning how to speak Spanish is one of the most valuable investments you can make.

Spanish School Evaluation Checklist

Name of school _____

Phone number _____

Address _____

Website _____

Criteria	Check	Notes
Good reviews online		
+/> 10 students in class		
Experienced teachers		
Students are like me		
Focus is on conversation		
Various levels offered		
Evaluation offered		
Location is reasonable		
Price is reasonable		

What do you like most about this school?

_____

_____

_____

What do you like least about this school?

_____

_____

_____

Do you believe that this school will successfully teach you how to speak Spanish?

_____

_____

_____

EASY STEP #4:

Practice every chance that you can

Wow! We are already up to Step 4!

You are doing so well. Now, what is it with us humans? We always like to over-complicate things and make them seem a lot harder than they need to be.

Spanish is no exception. There are thousands of words, phrases, grammar rules, and book after book, program after program, about 'the next big thing' in Spanish.

Yet where do we store (and use) all of this information? Is there really enough space in our heads to fully comprehend and get comfortable with this knowledge?

I've even met other Spanish professors that want it to be complicated - they think that by making the students work hard they will be better speakers. **But that is so wrong!**

My mission since I started teaching Spanish in 2005 has always been to make it easy and fun, and the best way to do that is to make friends with a Spanish speaker and practice.

Here's the deal. Spanish doesn't have to be hard. It doesn't have to be complex. **And you don't have to master it in order to start making friends and practicing!**

You'll get the most out of Spanish when you keep it simple and make it about the conversation, even if you can only speak a little bit! If you're new to Spanish, don't overwhelm yourself with complexity. Simply go out and find a Spanish speaker and start talking, even if you can only say a little.

You might be saying, I don't know anyone that speaks Spanish. I can almost guarantee you that you do - the United States is the melting pot of the world, and Spanish is taking over. There are now more Spanish speakers living in the United States than in any of the 20+ Spanish speaking countries in the world. As a matter of fact, the US is the largest Spanish speaking country in the world when you consider the total number of people that speak it.

Try this - at work tomorrow, start asking if anyone speaks Spanish or knows anyone that does. Or ask your neighbors and family members if they know any Spanish speakers. If that doesn't work, then go to your closest Mexican restaurant for lunch and ask your server.

I promise you that you will find someone that speaks Spanish, and that person would love to talk to you!

Once you have met someone, it gets easy. Use this simple introduction, and you will be speaking and having fun immediately:

- Hola, me llamo David. ¿Cómo te llamas?
- Soy de Estados Unidos. ¿De dónde eres?
- Estoy aprendiendo español. ¿Podemos practicar?

It is really this simple. The number one reason I have heard for not continuing with Spanish studies has been this very reason – I hear it over and over again: "I don't have anyone to practice with."

However, I don't understand it, because there are Spanish speakers everywhere. Think about it like this - just as bad as you want to practice Spanish, they want to practice English. So please, just try this simple suggestion. Go out and start talking!

You will be surprised at the opportunities there are to find yourself with someone that speaks Spanish. Here are some fun suggestions on the next few pages.

Activity 4

First, learn how to introduce yourself properly:

- Hola, me llamo David. ¿Cómo te llamas?
- Soy de Estados Unidos. ¿De dónde eres?
- Estoy aprendiendo español. ¿Podemos practicar?

Second, visit these places to practice:

Restaurants: Speak with the servers. Ask them for recommendations about the food and order it in Spanish. Ask them where they are from and what they like to do for fun.

Stores that you visit frequently: Introduce yourself. After meeting people, you can think about making small talk and asking them about things like music, sports, and the weather.

Bars/Cafés: Go in and order something to drink. If you see someone else, introduce yourself and offer him or her a beer or a cup of coffee.

If you can get comfortable introducing yourself in Spanish, you will be able to start speaking with people almost everywhere you go. It can be a little intimidating at first, but have fun with it and keep trying – every time it will get a little bit more comfortable and more enjoyable.

On the next few pages, I am including a few conversational activities from my book *"Let's Start Talking - A bilingual book for English and Spanish students"*, available on Amazon for $25.

I published this book to eliminate the fear that students have in conversing by giving them over 500 conversation starters. They are all available in both English and Spanish, so that you can practice Spanish and also help your conversation partner practice English.

Once you have your conversation partner, no matter what your level is, you can use these questions to make friendly conversation with Spanish speakers.

Preferences And Pleasures

1. Do you like to dance?
2. What is your favorite activity?
   a. Running
   b. Cooking
   c. Reading
   d. Skiing
   e. Traveling
   f. Going shopping
3. Do you like to read?
4. What kind of book do you prefer?
   a. Fiction
   b. Non-fiction
   c. Drama
   d. Comedy
   e. Mystery
   f. Science fiction
   g. Biography
5. Do you like dogs?
6. What is your favorite animal?
   a. Dogs
   b. Cats
   c. Fish
   d. Horses
   e. Rabbits
   f. Birds
7. Do you like funny movies?
8. What is your favorite movie?
   a. Comedies
   b. Romantic
   c. Drama
   d. Action
   e. Horror
9. Do you like sports?
10. What's your favorite team?

Preferencias y Placeres

1. ¿Te gusta bailar?
2. ¿Cuál es tu actividad favorita?
    a. Correr
    b. Cocinar
    c. Leer
    d. Esquiar
    e. Viajar
    f. Ir de compras
3. ¿Te gusta leer?
4. ¿Qué tipo de libro prefieres?
    a. Ficción
    b. No Ficción
    c. Drama
    d. Comedia
    e. Misterio
    f. Ciencia Ficción
    g. Biografías
5. ¿Te gustan los perros?
6. ¿Cuál es tu animal favorito?
    a. Los perros
    b. Los gatos
    c. Los peces
    d. Los caballos
    e. Los conejos
    f. Los aves
7. ¿Te gustan las películas cómicas?
8. ¿Cuál es tu película favorita?
    a. Las comedias
    b. Las románticas
    c. Las de drama
    d. Las de acción
    e. Las de horror
9. ¿Te gustan los deportes?
10. ¿Cuál es tu equipo favorito?

Your world

1. Do you have a boyfriend/girlfriend?
2. Do you have a special, weird, or useless talent?
3. What are the three most interesting things about you?
4. Do you have brothers or sisters?
5. Tell me about your family.
6. Do you have a car? What's it like?
7. Name 5 reasons that you are glad to be alive.
8. What are you the best at doing?
9. Do you live in a house or apartment? What's it like?
10. What is your favorite room? Why?
11. What clothes do you wear? What's it like?
12. Do you have a computer? What's it like?
13. Where is your favorite place to go for vacation?
14. Do you have a TV? What's it like?
15. What's your national flag like?
16. Do you have a watch? What's it like?
17. What is your favorite color? Why?
18. What makes you nervous?
19. Do you play a sport?
20. Do you play an instrument?
21. Tell me about your favorite activity.
22. Tell me about your job.
23. What is the best part about your job? What is the worst part?
24. What is your dream job?
25. What is your favorite song?

Tu mundo

1. ¿Tienes novio/novia?
2. ¿Tienes algún talento especial o fuera de lo común?
3. ¿Cuáles son las tres cualidades o virtudes que definen tu persona?
4. ¿Tienes hermanos?
5. Háblame un poco sobre tu familia.
6. ¿Tienes un carro? ¿Puedes describirlo?
7. Dime 5 razones por la cual disfrutas de la vida.
8. ¿En qué eres bueno?
9. ¿Vives en casa o apartamento? ¿Puedes describirla(o)?
10. ¿Cuál es tu habitación favorita en tu casa? ¿Por qué?
11. ¿Qué estilo de ropa te gusta vestir?
12. ¿Tienes una computadora? ¿Qué marca es?
13. ¿Cual está tu lugar favorito para ir de vacaciones?
14. ¿Tienes una televisión? ¿Puedes describirla?
15. ¿Puedes describir tu bandera nacional?
16. ¿Tienes un reloj?
17. ¿Cuál es tu color favorito? ¿Por qué?
18. ¿Qué te pone nervioso?
19. ¿Practicas algún deporte?
20. ¿Tocas algún instrumento musical?
21. Háblame un poco sobre tu actividad o pasatiempo favorito.
22. Háblame sobre tu trabajo.
23. ¿Qué te gusta más acerca de tu trabajo? ¿Qué no te gusta sobre tu trabajo?
24. ¿Cuál sería el tipo de trabajo ideal para ti o el de tus sueños?
25. ¿Cuál es tu canción favorita?

EASY STEP #5:

Find a conversation partner

I hope you are enjoying this book and have found my advice powerful and practical. Now for the final piece of advice – how to find a conversation partner!

There is no big mystery about this one - in order to achieve fluency you have to practice talking. Fluency originates from the Latin word fluentia, which means to flow. Think about a river... the water in a river flows downstream because the force of gravity outweighs any obstacle in its way. Speaking Spanish fluently means that there is nothing impeding your ability to speak it. In other words, you no longer have to think about it.

You might be thinking that it is impossible at this point, but I can tell you that if you get a conversation partner and meet with this person frequently, you will gradually eliminate your language barriers and the words will flow like the mighty Mississippi!

I know this is the case, because this is what I did. Below, I will tell you my story of living in Buenos Aires and how I met my conversation partner.

I met Socrates during my first immersion trip to Buenos Aires, Argentina during the summer of 2003. At this point I had been studying Spanish for a couple of years, but I still hadn't achieved what I would call real fluency.

I had spent so much time studying flashcards and had learned so much vocabulary, but I was missing this critical piece. I wasn't going out to talk with people.

Sure, I could understand a lot. And I had no problem getting around town, buying food and drinks, and going on guided tours of the city. And I was living with a retired housekeeper that enjoyed talking with me about the United States during dinner. This was a great way to practice, but unfortunately I didn't have a whole lot to talk about with an 80 year old lady, so I wanted more - I wanted to be friends with someone that I would normally be friends with. The catch was I was in Buenos Aires and I wanted this person to be a *"porteño"*, which is the Argentine word for a person from Buenos Aires.

The immersion school I was attending invited all of the students to an informal cocktail hour one evening, and most of the teachers and staff had invited their friends to come meet us.

After serving some light snacks and Malbec, we began intermingling and talking to each other. One thing that almost all of the *"porteños"* had in common was that they were studying English and thrilled to meet people they could practice with.

Socrates and I began to talk, and really hit it off. I thought his English was phenomenal, and he taught me a lot of new words and the real way that people talked. You see, text book Spanish and conversational Spanish are not always the same. In fact, most people, including you and me, use a lot of slang and other idiomatic expressions, and these are rarely taught in a book. You have to really talk to people to get it!

Talking with Socrates made me feel really good and I started getting confident in my conversational abilities, because we went so much deeper than the normal introductions that night. We talked about sports and politics, our family and friends, and our plans for the future. And the coolest part - he could understand me, and I could understand him! Sometimes we switched over to English, and at other times we spoke pure Spanish, but we communicated very effectively.

I felt great talking to Socrates, so I suggested that we try to get together more frequently to practice. We started by meeting at the "Shopping" (the argentine word for mall) after my classes and on his lunch break, and ended up doing this almost everyday for the next two weeks. He invited me to watch the "fútbol" games with his friends and showed me all around town.

Socrates taught me a lot, and we became very good friends. He is still the first person I look up when I go back to Argentina, and since the year of 2003 he never forgets to send me a message on my birthday.

You see, this is what learning how to speak Spanish is all about. It's usually not about the language, or the grammar. It's not based on a textbook or a classroom.

It's about getting out there and putting yourself into what might be initially uncomfortable situations, but meeting new people and making connections that last a lifetime.

You may already be an expert Spanish speaker or someone that is just starting, but my final piece of advice is so valuable if you act on it. It should be really easy to do if you are on an immersion trip, but there is really no travel required.

The United States is full of people coming from Latin America and more and more are arriving everyday. From what I have seen, Spanish speakers are some of the friendliest people in the world, and they are dying to make friends with Americans so they can practice English.

The next time you hear someone speaking Spanish, smile and introduce yourself in Spanish. Let him or her know that you want to practice and help with English too. With this simple act of kindness, you might just make your new best friend, or even meet the man or woman that you eventually fall in love with and marry.

There are very few things that you can do that can make this type of impact on your life, and speaking Spanish can help you make more money, experience the world, and truly change your life forever.

That's it from me for now. Make sure to refer to the following pages for the final activity and worksheets to learn how to find and work with a practice partner.

I love to hear from my students, so if you have found this useful, please leave a comment on The Language School's Facebook page. Here is the link:

https://www.facebook.com/TheLanguageSchool/

Finally, please let your friends and family know about this awesome program.

Activity 5

Spanish speakers are everywhere!!! To find one, try these ideas:

1. Ask your friends and family if they speak Spanish or can introduce you to someone that does.

2. Post to Facebook, Twitter, LinkedIn, or any other social media account you use that you need a Spanish-speaking conversation partner.

3. Visit restaurants - Mexican, Cuban, Peruvian, etc.

4. Look for a cultural center or non-profit focused on Spanish speakers.

5. Go to the library and ask about Spanish or English conversation groups.

6. Volunteer at a public school to help tutor ESL or literacy.

7. Sign up for Latin dance classes like Tango or Salsa.

8. Sign up for a dating site like Match.com.

9. Apply for a job at a company with a multicultural workforce.

10. Register with Meetup.com.

Rules of engagement:

Not everyone will be a good conversation partner – so make sure that you follow this advice. First and foremost, introduce yourself to people that you hear speaking Spanish. Make the first move to make them feel comfortable.

Your conversation partner needs to be someone safe to talk to that will encourage you and make you feel good, using simple and easy phrases to help you understand and gradually adding complexity as you go.

Rules for working with conversation partners

1. The best conversation partners are also studying a language, preferably your native language. Then it will be an equal exchange!

2. Your own classmates may be great partners too – if you can maintain the conversation in Spanish.

3. Spouses and children rarely make a good conversation partner.

4. Your partner should be someone that you feel comfortable with in the first place.

5. He or she should always try to understand what you mean.

6. They don't always need to correct your mistakes.

7. Make sure that you listen as much as you talk and repeat what you hear.

8. Take baby steps – simple conversations are good.

9. Get together frequently – daily if possible. Organize meetings around safe topics of conversation and talk about things you like.

10. Meet somewhere conducive to conversation. Coffee is always a good idea!

IN CONCLUSION

I wrote this book because I have been learning and teaching people how to speak new languages since 2001, and I have helped so many people make real progress with this advice. In recent years I have recognized a strong need to develop easy to follow programs that make learning fun and make it about the conversation, not the grammar. But I have also recognized a need to teach my students how to study Spanish and how to practice it so that they can get real results.

Over the years I have heard so many comments from my students that they really want to make friends with native speakers of the languages they are learning, but they don't know where to start. This short and simple book is packed with advice to help you learn Spanish by teaching you how to study it and how to find someone that you can practice with.

You have to find a great program that will teach you Spanish that is relevant to your goals, which is why you learned how to write about your objectives and inspiration in step 1 of this book. In the second step I teach you how to make it easy by initially only trying to learn 10 new words a day – don't over complicate this! If you learn 10 new words every day, in only 3 months you should know enough Spanish to converse in most of your daily interactions with Spanish speakers.

Now, step 3 is really important, because you have to find a good program to help you through this process. As the director of The Language School I get asked daily how much the classes cost, but this question really does nothing to tell you if the program will work for you, which is why I created the questionnaire to help you ask the right questions. Outside of learning Spanish, steps 4 and 5 are critical, because you have to find someone that you can practice with. You need to make your Spanish studies about speaking Spanish with real people. Once you start speaking it, the real fun begins, and you will be so glad that you started learning how to speak Spanish.

We are living in interesting times, and despite all of the positive progress we have made as a country, our communities are still divided because of skin color, cultural differences, and language barriers. I want to do everything I can to help people break down these language and cultural barriers, and I firmly believe that if we can teach Spanish speakers English and English speakers Spanish, the United States will continue to be the most powerful nation in the world and the best place to live and work.

Likewise, I think if we don't do this and people continue to live in segmented communities, we are on the brink of disaster. Many people are angry and in this election year of 2016, at the time that I am writing this book, I am seeing stories on the news every day of people being harassed and violently attacked. Many people are worried that they will soon be deported and separated from their friends and family. A lot of these people have lived here for most of their lives and would be in a terrible situation if they were to get deported. But they are facing a terrifying time now because their parents, at no fault of their own, brought them here to grow up out of desperation.

The Language School is dedicated to this mission of bringing together English and Spanish speakers, and that's why we only teach these two languages, because the United States is facing a crisis – an identity and cultural crisis that is ruining people's lives.

I never would have thought that running a language school and teaching people new languages could be so controversial, but unfortunately I get a lot of messages and hear commentary all too frequently, especially from Americans, that we don't need to learn Spanish and people immigrating to this country need to learn English.

I agree that if people are planning on moving to this country, they should make learning English and the American culture part of their daily routine, and from what I see they do. But right now there is so much hate and hostility in the air that is coming from misunderstandings and political manipulations of the American public.

We need to change as a culture and as a country and remember where we came from. We need to remember that most of us also come from other countries and we need to be more supportive of those that don't have any choice but to move here.

Many people aren't necessarily planning on moving here – in fact, the vast majority of my English students have informed me they moved here out of necessity. I have students that are here on political asylum because corrupt politicians have threatened their families because they know information that would be harmful to the rich and powerful politicians. I have many other students that no matter how hard they look for work in their home country, they can't find it. Unfortunately they have families to support and have to come to the US looking for better opportunities. Another fairly large percentage of my students is made up of honest people that have found themselves cross with the drug cartels and have had to flee for safety reasons.

The United States of America is the greatest country in the world, but the reason why is because it is a unique idea of a country that has always been open to immigration. It was founded by people leaving European countries for many of the same reasons our Spanish-speaking neighbors are moving here and has always been a welcoming country for those looking for life, liberty, and the pursuit of happiness. By learning Spanish, you can actually have a tremendous impact on those looking to learn English, and then we both win.

I have a special interest in helping teachers, healthcare personnel, and emergency responders. You see, the US is now the largest Spanish speaking country in the world, and despite people's best efforts to learn English, there is still a very large quantity of Spanish speaking people that need extra help. And remember, it takes time, so people that have recently arrived need some time to learn English.

The teachers in our communities with non-English speaking students are really struggling, and the rest of the students are struggling because of this. Police, fire fighters, and emergency medical technicians tell me everyday that speaking Spanish can be the difference between life and death.

Learning Spanish is such a great thing to do, and will have a great impact on your life, both professionally and personally. Good luck, and don't hesitate to contact me with any questions, comments, or concerns on our Facebook page at the following link:

https://www.facebook.com/TheLanguageSchool/

I greatly appreciate you taking the time to read this book and your interest in learning Spanish. If more people would take the time to learn Spanish, I think our communities would be much safer and happier places.